Be You Nique:

A Book of Memes and Posts

Be You Nique:

A Book of Memes and Posts

Nadia Atkinson

BeYOUnique

Be You Nique Publishing

Be You Nique: A Book of Memes and Posts
By Nadia Atkinson
Published by Be You Nique Publishing
www.beyoutimes2.com

Cover art work by Nadia Atkinson
Printed in the United States of America

DEDICATION

This book is dedicated to all of the men and women who follow me on Facebook, Instagram, Twitter, and any other social media platforms that I share my opinions with you.

Thank you for keeping me sharp and humbled.

This one's for you!

June 29, 2013

Sometimes I do things that I'm not proud of. Other times I feel my baby steps turn into sprints. Today the one thing I can say for sure is, today is today and yesterday was a day that I can never take back. I cannot change the things that were done but I can change the things I am not proud of today.

INSTANT GRATIFICATION ONLY WORKS IF YOU DON'T CARE HOW THE
JOB GETS DONE.
EVERYTHING IS ABOUT PROCESS.
YOU CAN'T WANT THE BILLION DOLLAR BUSINESS WITHOUT GOING
THROUGH A PROCESS.
GOD WILL OPEN DOORS THAT SEEM SHUT AFTER GOING THROUGH A
PROCESS.
INSTANT GRATIFICATION + GOD DOESN'T WORK.
BUT,
FAITH + PROCESS =
PROGRESS
#BEYOUNIQUE

July 15, 2013

Sometimes you just have to look the devil in the face and tell him that he is a liar and he has already been defeated so he cannot win ever! We are the head and not the tail! I have gained everlasting life! You were thrown out of heaven! Stop trying to bring me down with you! I cannot stand for it! I will not stand for it! And I am soooooo tired of! My God reigns forever and forever amen!

—feeling loved.

The most attractive thing a man could ever be to me is: sensitive.
You don't always have to be strong and macho.
Tell me your fears, let's discuss vision and show vulnerability.
Stop worrying about appearing weak because once you do the above she'll automatically see you as strong.
#beyounique
<3

July 29, 2013

"People are our sunshine, our soil, our rain. When are we going to stop surviving off of people and start living for ourselves?" - Nadia A.

—😛 feeling strong

August 16, 2013

"For He made Him who knew no sin to be sin for us, that we might become the righteousness of God in Him." (II Corinthians 5:21 NKJV)

Jesus became what He hated the most (sin) for us!!! How can you not take a few seconds to THANK HIM for what He has done for you? Jesus didn't die on the cross as Jesus, He died as me! (And you) Thank you Lord!!!

August 29, 2013

"Worry is a choice that displeases God. When you worry, you reveal that you don't really trust God to provide all that you need." - June Hunt

Saw this in my bible during service tonight! I worried about everything all the time then I realized I don't have to control everything now and fifteen days from now. I need to learn to live for today! (Matt. 6:34) So, I share this with all 500+ of you Facebook friends of mine and I pray it blesses you as it did me. Good night! Let the midnight packing begin!

SOCIETY WANTS YOU TO BELIEVE YOU'RE NOT GOOD ENOUGH.
I WANT YOU TO BELIEVE YOU'RE GREATER THAN SOCIETY,
YOUR WORST ENEMY, AND THE PERSON IN YOUR MIND
TELLING YOU THAT YOUR LIFE ISN'T WORTH LIVING.
EMBRACE WHO YOU ARE.
YOU'RE THE ONLY ONE WHO WILL BELIEVE IT.
#BEYOUNIQUE

September 4, 2013

It's amazing how some of us can text faster than we can type; but won't take a few seconds to encourage someone. it takes less than a minute to text someone saying "hey, I miss you, I love you, you're awesome, I'm proud of you, thinking about you, God loves you, keep up the great work, I can't wait to see you, you're wonderful, beautiful, etc". These quick words of encouragement can change a person's entire day or it can allow them to zone out for 30 seconds to say to themselves wow someone cares. So, I challenge everyone to take 20 seconds to encourage the first person that comes to mind to brighten up their day.

September 12, 2013

I am sooooo not a morning person but I find myself awake at 4 am on a daily basis. I can honestly say that I am grateful for this phase of my life because I am starting to believe that if I am asleep, the work that I am supposed to do for my Fathers Kingdom will not get done. My book is due out next month and I am extremely excited. I've been waiting so long for this and it's almost here. Thank you Lord for the deposits that you are making. All the glory belongs to you! Big spiritual hugs and kisses!

—😊 feeling determined.

September 16, 2013

God's intention in allowing testing is to prove strength of character; Satan's intention is to prove lack of character.

Don't let Satan attack you like He attacked Job's character. Stay close to God. Continue to pray and read his word! Better days are coming!

"For no temptation (no trial regarded as enticing to sin), [no matter how it comes or where it leads] has overtaken you and laid hold on you that is not common to man [that is, no temptation or trial has come to you that is beyond human resistance and that is not adjusted and adapted and belonging to human experience, and such as man can bear]. But God is faithful [to His Word and to His compassionate nature], and He [can be trusted] not to let you be tempted and tried and assayed beyond your ability and strength of resistance and power to endure, but with the temptation He will [always] also provide the way out (the means of escape to a landing place), that you may be capable and strong and powerful to bear up under it patiently." (1 Corinthians 10:13 AMP)

WHEN YOU TAKE A LOOK AT YOUR CIRCLE,
ARE THE FIVE PEOPLE CLOSEST TO YOU
HELPING YOU OR HURTING YOU?
THINK ABOUT IT.
#BEYOUNIQUE

October 16, 2013

Children of God don't need luck. We're already covered!! Thanks.#thatisall

October 20, 2013

My past does not define me! You cannot move closer to your destiny if you're still holding on
to your past. Let it go! That may include family and friends. Just let go and let God!
Coincidently or not... my book is called The Past is in the Past so let it Pass!
Let is pass and move FORWARD!
It is possible I am proof!
Enjoy your Sunday people!

The PAST is in the PAST so let it PASS

FOR WOMEN

By Nadia Atkinson

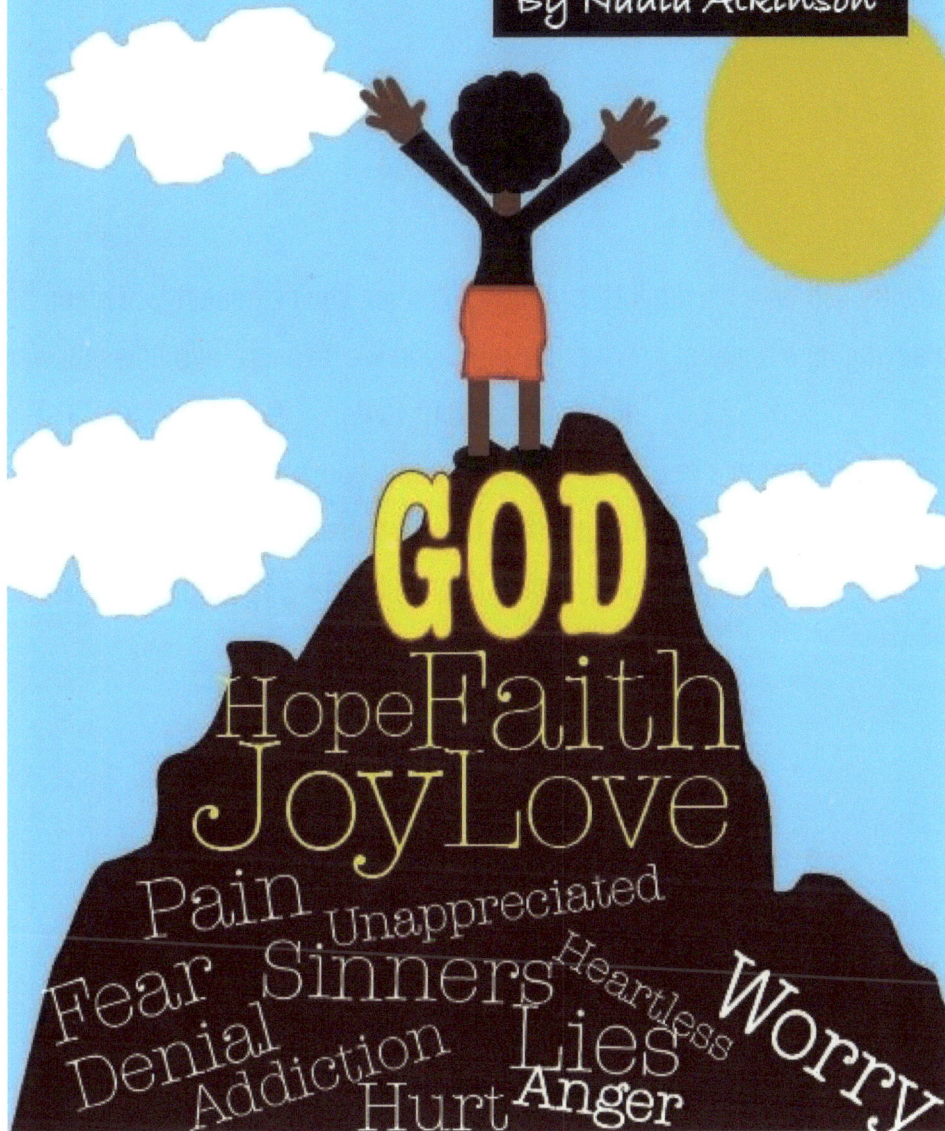

GOD

HopeFaith
JoyLove

Pain Unappreciated
Fear Sinners Heartless Worry
Denial Addiction Lies
Hurt Anger

October 25, 2013

I know honesty can be a hard pill to swallow but when you're honest you sleep better at night. Stop saving face and just be you! Say what you want to say, live how you want to live, do what you want to do.
We're here to please one person and you know who it is.
Honesty is the best policy. Some people may take it as being harsh but not everyone is as strong as you are. It's okay they will thank you later. Gn

There are two types of people...
The ones who make things happen and
The ones who watch people make things happen.
Guess which one I am?
Now think about which one you are.
Put your dreams into motion NOW!
#beyounique

October 28, 2013

I want to stay true to myself. I want to be the best woman I can be.
A woman of strength, smarts, and love covered by the blood of Jesus.
No weapon formed against me shall prosper. So take a number because with the armor I'm packing you'll be waiting a long time to try and get to me!

#onmyjourney #covered #power #strength #iamwoman #isaiah54:17

Be blessed today!

LOCKED

FROM THE MOMENT WE LOCKED EYES I KNEW MY FUTURE WOULD BE
NOTHING SHORT OF BLISS.
I SAW YOU, ME, THEN WE. MY FUTURE THAT ONCE CONSISTED OF
ONLY ME, NOW INCLUDED YOU AND A PARTY OF TWO.
IN A WORLD OF CHAOS YOU ARE THE EYE OF THE STORM AND ALL I
WANTED TO KNOW IS WHY IT TOOK YOU SO LONG...

#BEYOUNIQUE

October 30, 2013

Boy meets girl. Girl meets boy. Boy falls in love with girl. Girl falls in love with boy. Cute right? Then...
They start listening to what everyone else has to say about their relationship instead of remembering the
simple things like when boy fell in love with girl and girl fell in love with boy.
Stop!
Don't complicate love. If you love him or her don't let anyone get in between the love you have for one
another. Not your parents, brothers, sisters, aunts, uncles, cousins, friends, no one!
Just stick it out and do it for love. It's what some of our parents did, right?

Let's get back to that...

November 3, 2013

Many of you are sitting on ideas that you believe are like someone else's. Many of you fail to realize that your thoughts are just that, YOUR thoughts. It's time to take a leap of faith and put those ideas into motion.
I surround myself with young entrepreneurs not purposely but because we realize that we are unique and we are too smart to sit back and let our great minds go to waste.
We encourage one another to start our own businesses and we know we are the future of America.
Take a leap of faith and allow this year to be your year of breakthrough!
Nadia

November 25, 2013

Trusting someone can be hard.

Loving someone can be even more difficult.

But, knowing that you can trust in God because God is love.

Now that is priceless.

God wants to help get to that next step.
The question is:
Why are you running?
#beyounique

November 26, 2013

Sometimes in my mind I have it all figured out. Then I dream a dream and God changes all that I figured out. It is up to me to go with my plan or God's plan. I chose God's plan. Did I want to? No. I know it will be for the better. Obedience is key. But, first you must discern and pray.

Follow your dreams... literally.

January 22, 2014

Today I encourage you to look through your cell phone and delete the photos that no longer define the season you are in.

I am big on quotes. I believe there are so many a-ha moments from quotes but there were way too many in my phone that reminded me of a dry season.

It's time to change your life all around. Make today the day you decide to no longer live in the past and allow your today to be better than yesterday.

Don't wait on God to take you out of your season. Be proactive and turn your season around with God. He wants to see you grow not sulk. Continue to rely on His word. Tell Him you need to hear from Him. Open His word and ask Him to guide you to a scripture of encouragement.

Today I refuse to be in a lowly place for I am a child of the Most High God and I will overcome!!!

Amen.

Make today the day you get one step closer to your goal.
Don't give up.
Everything you need to achieve your goal has already been placed
around you.
God is the M. D. 'Master Designer' of all things. Trust me if you ask
the right questions, do the right things, you'll get the right answers.
#beyounique

January 24, 2014

Dear Summer,

Hi remember me? It's your favorite beach girl! You know the one who wears socks to run across the hot sand. Lol Anyway, I was hoping we could make a deal. I won't complain if we have as many hella hot days this summer if you can come a little early this year in exchange for these negative temps this winter!

Please don't make me beg!!

Your #1 fan,

Nadie La

January 25, 2014

I love who I have become, I love who I will be. If my life right now is a glimpse of where I am going, then I will continue to be all that I can be.

<3 Nadia

Have a great weekend!!

Love is....

Speechless
Timeless
Complicated
Limitless
Fear
Mesmerizing
Euphoric
God

... All of these things

WE SERVE AN IMPOSSIBLE GOD. HE MAKES DREAMS YOU'VE NEVER IMAGED COME TRUE.
#ONLYGOD #MARVELED #BEYOUNIQUE

January 27, 2014

In the end it was always Him and I.
As long as I am focused on Him my paths will always be straight.
The adversary will do whatever he can to try to steer you off of your path. But God! He is faithful.
Do not give way to the devil. He's a certified clown and liar and I do not have tolerance for such this year! It's go time!!!

Make it a great day!

February 2, 2014

Someone said to me today that I look like my joy has returned. I had to let that sink in because I never really knew it was gone. Situations may occur where you don't realize it has/had left until someone mentions it to you. This video made me think wow I am happy I am back to my old self. I guess she was missed by many and I'm glad because I missed her too. Get back to the things that bring you joy.

When you're disobedient to God by not following the path He gave you, you will continue to go down the wrong path making your current situation worse. When you follow His voice and walk down the right path He will prosper you.

'Hope deferred makes the heart sick, But when the desire comes, it is a tree of life.' (Proverbs 13:12 NKJV)

It's simple: stop wasting your time complaining about where you are now and do something about it.

Faith without works is dead.

#beyounique

February 17, 2014

When someone doesn't believe in you and openly professes it to you... It's only adding fuel to the fire. You can say thank you by showing them.
The unbelief that they had in you should never trump the vision God put in you.

He says I can do it, therefore I will do it.

#hihaters #byehaters #myGodisbigger #icandoallthings #newyearnewme #nevertoolatetofinish

February 27, 2014

Many of you are on Facebook openly complaining about life. So many people are just upset with the way things are in their life. But I just want to share something with anyone reading this message... Google "how many people died today?" Click on the first link and it will give you real time numbers of how many people have lost their lives today! As of 2:37 pm ET 95,771 people have lost their lives today and the day isn't over yet. You are upset about something so small. God woke you up today. He sent down angels to protect you overnight so you could wake up in the morning. Have you thanked Him for doing that yet?

When God looks at you He doesn't see your religion, He sees your heart.

🙌🙌🙌🙌🙌

Be**YOU**nique

#beyounique

March 3, 2014

Lupita Nyong'o said in an interview that as a kid people would tease her and call her the girl with 'dark night skin'. She went on to say that she prayed daily for God to make her beautiful. Every morning she woke up rushing to the mirror to check (I am sure of it). Who wouldn't if your faith is that real in Something so big as God?

God is a God of impossible. Lupita in a million years never guessed she would be a model and OSCAR award winning actress. Her look is so edgy and captivating that you can't help but to stare into her eyes and wonder where she's been hiding because of her beauty.

It may have taken 20+ years of prayer but one day she woke up and she was the most beautiful girl in the world. That is impossible to a 7 year old girl who was teased about her beauty.

Two lessons in this... Never stop praying. God hears our prayers the first time we ask for something. He will always show up and show out! Second, God is the God of impossible. Whatever you believe is your biggest dream, it's going to be bigger! You can't think of it. You can't understand just how big you can be but our God in Heaven knows.

Never stop praying and start getting excited for what God is about to do in your life! Congratulations to Lupita for winning an Oscar tonight. She deserves every award for an outstanding role. God bless her and you!

Nadia Atkinson

YOUR LIFE MAY NOT BE EASY. IN FACT, YOUR LIFE MAY HAVE NEVER BEEN EASY BUT TRUST IN THE LORD WITH ALL OF YOUR HEART. HE IS PERFECTING YOUR CONCERNS. GOD WILL NEVER TURN BACK ON HIS WORD. TRUST HIM.
HE IS FAITHFUL!
#BEYOUNIQUE

March 12, 2014

In my bedroom I have this quote to remind me to enjoy life. It goes perfect with this devotional...

"Never get so BUSY making a LIVING that you FORGET to make a LIFE."

Enjoy!! Be blessed today as you go out into the world. Try to break your "routine" and do something different today. Smile, laugh, sing out loud in your car, call someone you haven't spoken to in a while, hold the door for a stranger even if they are 500 feet away. Do something different. You'll be glad you did. - nma

It's OK to Enjoy Your Life

March 13, 2014

The grind is real!!!!!!! I've been non-stop all week but the reward is coming!!!

Persistence is key.

Best wishes to those who are finishing up midterms this week.

Remember, never give power to those who talk bad about you. Instead show them love and then kindly direct them to stophating.com ☺ lol be blessed y'all!

Sometimes you have to let God give you those valleys to get to the next victory!
What do I mean by give you those valleys?
You have to embrace what God has given you. Prove to him that you trust him enough to not disappoint him.
Everything happens for a reason. Don't give up!
With much pressure a diamond eventually forms.
#beyounique

March 16, 2014

Your life may not be easy. In fact, your life may have never been easy but, trust in The Lord with all of your heart. He is perfecting your concerns. God will never turn back on His Word.
Trust Him. He is faithful.
#beyounique
Be blessed on this amazing day!

March 30, 2014

I wanted to remind both men and women alike that God made us in His image as Genesis 1:27 mentions, not anyone else. Hence, the Be You Nique, LLC logo which emphasizes a fingerprint. I feel that social media has tainted this for both the believer and the non-believer. What I mean by that is so many people wear masks and are starting to believe their own lies and the representation of their representative. I personally just want to be me and be free happily living for Christ. I want the same for others. There's nothing wrong with social media; it is only wrong when people know the REAL you and you keep posting lies. Please, please, please continue to BE YOU and don't worry about what the next man thinks. Just be you nique. It is really that simple.

The fact that you have a
fingerprint that doesn't match
anyone else's... You are set
apart by God to fulfill a destiny
designed solely for you.
Don't let YOUR Father down.
#beyounique

April 3, 2014

Sometimes the unbelievable truth is just that, unbelievable. But, when it comes to love, unbelief can be beautiful.

I have no clue what I just wrote but I know that my Heavenly Father says I am loved therefore you are.

Have a blessed day!

April 4, 2014

Life: it can go in two directions. for better or for worse. Many believe that their life is always going in the opposite direction, for the worse. I see and hear people say FML (sorry) or I hate my life for the stupidest things yet you only have one.

Yes, we all have bad days but most importantly it's up to you to allow that bad situation to ruin your entire day.
Nowadays, I tell people make it a great day, make it an amazing day, or be blessed on this amazing day. You are in charge of the outcome of your day.
Yesterday, many employees cried to me in confidence, yesterday my teacher forgot to tell me I needed an appointment to take a midterm therefore I couldn't take it, yesterday I needed to be in the Lords house but I decided to assist family instead, yesterday it was 65 degrees and I was at work all day and couldn't enjoy it, yesterday all of these unexpected occurrences gave me a pounding headache along with a few other things. I was upset for ten minutes I won't lie but I didn't let it steal my joy!

Thank God today for opening your eyes and declare that today will be a good day. You control the outcome and stop saying your life sucks because when you look at the small positives they make this life worth it.

Many blessings to you and go out and make today great!!

I 💜 Me...
First.
The others? Well...they will just have to wait.
When your love is given, give it in it's purest form. However, not everyone is ready to receive it. There's always an excuse as to why they aren't ready to receive it. Yet, they are the ones who exuded it first in their purest form. When they have you where they want you then it's time to press the breaks. ✋

Let's do us both a favor and continue to love in the purest form because if your wall goes up the only one who will going to hurt the most is you.

#beyounique

April 6, 2014

Knowing. Understanding. Realize. Growing.

When you KNOW something is bad for you, it's up to you to decide if it/they should remain in your life.

When you UNDERSTAND why something is bad for you, after all the negative that this thing has caused you, you REALIZE you should've let that thing go a long time ago. Instead you went down a long, dreadful path of pain, suffering, turmoil, and headaches. But, once you finally let that thing go... Time passes and that thing you knew was so bad for you, suddenly causes you to GROW and become a better person. You're now ready for the next phase of your life.

This thing we call "free will" is real. Know that the Holy Spirit in you or your gut tells you when to stop and go. Understand that God gave us this gift to guide us in life. Realize that It is here to help us grow from faith to faith.

The question is will you listen?

April 13, 2014

Lately I've been so busy that I tend to put off things that should be done. However, at the time they were not of importance so I didn't address them. But let me tell you how awesome God is. He sends people to me to inquire about those same tasks who have the right people in line to complete them for me. What?!? I can't be more ecstatic about God.

That's why I can never be too busy for Him. He takes care of me always!!!

April 14, 2014

As women we are so hard on ourselves that we forget God created us in His image which is beyond beautiful. Know, understand, and appreciate your beauty. Don't try and be like the next woMan.

Just #beyounique

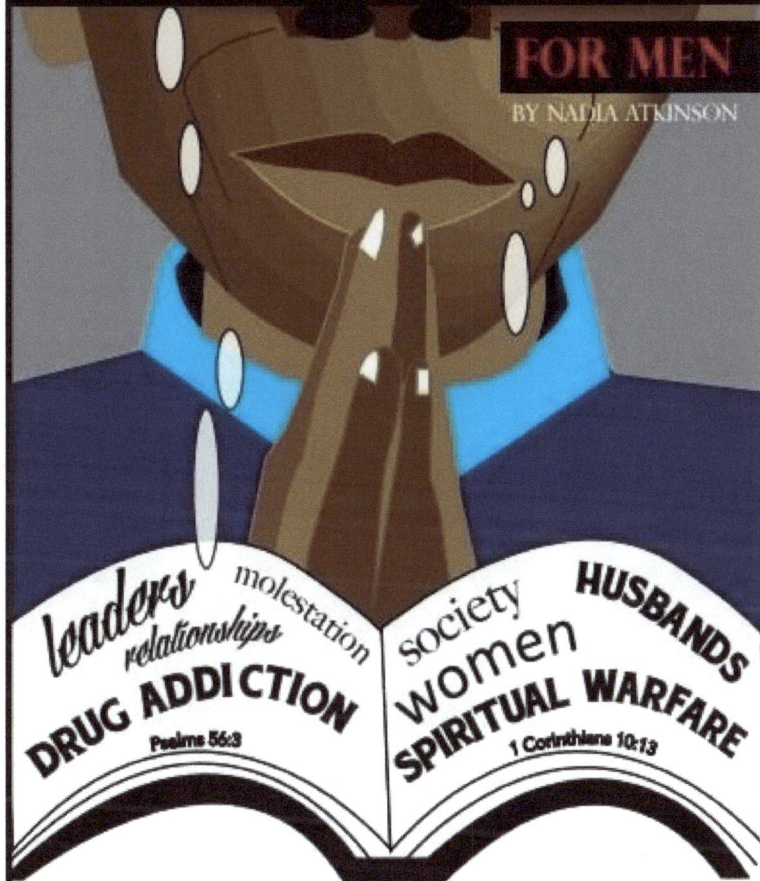

Fight for what you want.
That includes the guy or girl that doesn't know what they want.
Let's make something clear...
If you want me, you have to earn me.

April 22, 2014

Thanking God for the opportunities that today may offer.

I pray He opens my eyes and ears to see and hear the things that are of Him to know He is with me and will continue to answer my prayers. I pray for my family this morning that we all wake in Jesus name. I pray for my friends and the people I haven't met yet who are apart of making my destiny and journey what God intended it to be. I pray for mental clarity and peace during these times, wisdom, and love to be more like You. I pray that anyone reading this prayer desires the same in Jesus name, Amen.

Today go into the world and know you are loved, appreciated, and adored by the Most High. He makes all things new, never give up because breakthrough is right around the corner. When you serve the author of time, all things work together for good. Be patient. I have too many blessings to tell you about and not enough time. He is sooooo good. Be patient. It's life's greatest lesson.

Make it a great day!!

Nadia

April 27, 2014

The thought that God loves us, knows us, and our FUTURE. He still loves the atheist who claims there is no God! Wow!

He already knew that! That's mind blowing to me. I don't know about you!

#Godisawesome

April 30, 2014

Wow this shut me up!

Finally, brethren, whatever things are true, whatever things are noble, whatever things are just, whatever things are pure, whatever things are lovely, whatever things are of good report, if there is any virtue and if there is anything praiseworthy—meditate on these things. (Philippians 4:8 NKJV)

Have a blessed day!!

May 4, 2014

Each and every day I can think about three things that I constantly want to change. I can do one of two things: I can let these negative things bring me down or I can wait on The Lord. I don't know what it is about the week of May 11th but so many great things are happening that week for me and I have to continue to believe that they will continue.

Happiness starts within. If you allow negative thoughts to sprout in your mind eventually they will start to grow roots and branches. Kill them before they grow through much prayer and using the Word of God. If you know the kind of Father you have then you know He only wants good for you.

Once you receive this revelation it is pretty difficult to not be happy.

The more I grow in Christ the happier I become. I know that song by Pharrell is annoying to some right now but that song had everyone in the best mood when you first heard it. That needs to be the soundtrack of your life.

We as humans believe material things and people make us happy. But, when you truly think about it does it really? One is never satisfied with these things 90% of the time. If left alone for too long negative thoughts start to take over your mind. When this happens pray, sing Pharrell, read the word, do a quick dance, or think of something positive you accomplished lately. Change your heart and change your mind.

It all starts with you. For God is perfecting your concerns (psalms 138:8) Trust in the Lord with all your heart, And lean not on your own understanding; In all your ways acknowledge Him, And He shall direct your paths. (Proverbs 3:5,6)

And do not be conformed to this world, but be transformed by the renewing of your mind, that you may prove what is that good and acceptable and perfect will of God. (Romans 12:2)

Have an awesome Sunday!!

#beyounique

May 30, 2014

Yesterday I was listening to a sermon by Pastor Steve Furtick and the one thing he kept emphasizing is that we are easily distracted.
At times I think of how much work really goes into putting out the next book title and I don't want to do it. Then I think about this childhood dream I had and how I wanted to own my own publishing company. Now that I do, I am acting like I don't appreciate what God has blessed me with due to various distractions.
I can no longer allow distractions to hinder God given seeds that will never see fruition due to my lack of focus. Please stay focused on your goals.
I want to thank the prayer warriors who continuously keep me in prayer because they see something in me. I don't want to name drop but thank you!
I don't care about me putting my business out there. When you're in the position I am in and you're trying to achieve the goals I am trying to achieve, transparency is key.
Have a blessed day.
With God all things are possible.

DON'T FALL IN LOVE WITH THE POSSIBILITY OF WHAT
COULD BE.
FALL IN LOVE WITH WHAT IS.
IF IT ISN'T WHAT YOU WANT THEN IT'S TIME TO GO.
#IJS
#BEYOUNIQUE

June 6, 2014

Think about it. When you're constantly trying to please people you're stressed. When you're trying to please God and only God; life is easy squeezy. This morning's devotional made me reflect on my childhood and how I always wanted to fit in until I didn't anymore. I surrounded myself with a group of people who stood out and we named ourselves 'The Sophisticated Ladies'. My point is when you stop trying to be like everyone else God changes you internally. He heals you of that mindset and shows you the benefits of pleasing Him. Do that for the next 30 days. Make it a habit and watch the doors that will open.

Have a blessed day and enjoy your weekend!!

'Listen to what he does and watch what he says'
One of the best books I have ever read. Your words have to line up with your actions. If they don't then I am 💯% sure I will start to question everything that you have ever done and said due to you not being consistent. Words are powerful people. Pay attention, don't allow your head to get all caught up in the clouds.

June 13, 2014

So many people are dealing with these issues presently. Cast your cares upon The Lord... For He is perfecting our concerns. (My fave) It's tough to let the past go but take it from me, a woman who titled her book after the past, leave it in the past. You cannot reap the benefits and rewards of a door that God is trying to open for you if you have the last door cracked open. Close it. You obviously departed from that thing because it was no longer serving it's purpose in your life. Today I decree and declare that your past will no longer be a setback but a set up for your come back! In Jesus mighty name, Amen!

June 17, 2014

It's so important to write stuff down. If you were given a vision and you expect to remember it, you won't. In November 2011, I made a vision book then in February 2013 I made a faith board. I found my vision book from Nov 2011; the craziest thing is some things in that book are starting to happen now and other things already happened and have phased themselves out. My point is if you don't have a constant reminder of what it is God is expecting you to do how will you ever do them? We often get sidetracked by the daily happenings of life but I encourage you to stay focused on your dreams, visions, and goals. You can't expect to get there overnight but keep fighting for them. Put in the work because eventually they will come to Pass.

June 20, 2014

When you see it, you'll know it. When you feel it, you'll know it. When you find it, you won't lose it. But, if it's not meant... all you can do is let it go. Your time will come. Until then keep pushing for your goals and draw closer to God.

#singleladies #singlegents #reachforGodslove #loveistrue #loveisblind #Godsloveiseternal

Good night ladies n gents

When you are confident in who you are, there will always be someone in your corner telling you that you can't be great. Do me a favor and keep going. They can't do it so they believe you can't.
#beyounique

June 27, 2014

I just want to remind someone that God is able! We serve a limitless God. He is the God of impossible.

Think back to your childhood, think of all the dreams you once had and see if those things are coming to past. If not do what you can to achieve them.

Children are special to God and He gives us these dreams to achieve them all the while His glory is shining through you! Don't allow Satan to be a dream thief. Prove him wrong! We have six months before the year is over. Let's think about those childhood dreams and put them into action. I am, I have, and will continue to do so; now it's your turn!

June 30, 2014

Many individuals want to have a huge circle of friends but it's always better to have a few true friends than a bunch you can't trust. #quality #quantity #loyalty #friendship #lifeoverlove #beyou #beyoutimes2

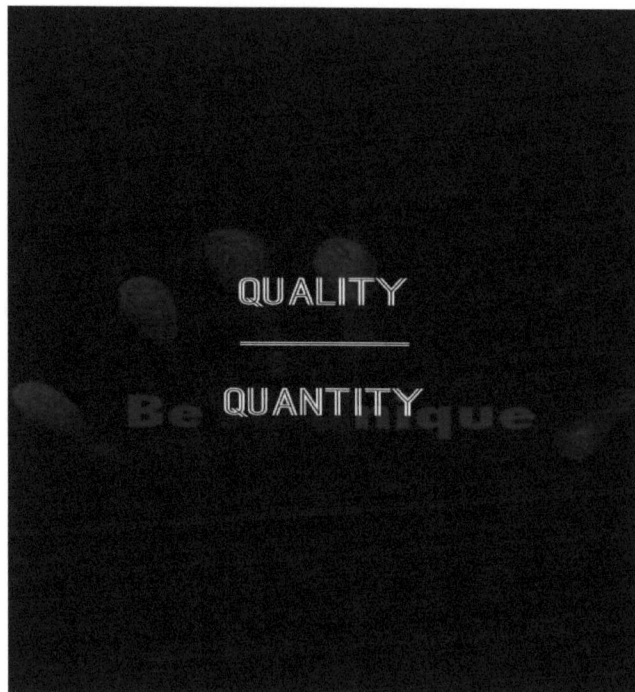

July 1, 2014

Cherish it. Never let anyone steal your joy especially when He is the one who gives it to you!

#beyounique

YOUR RELATIONSHIP WITH GOD IS JUST THAT...
YOUR RELATIONSHIP.
NEVER LET ANYONE TAKE THAT AWAY FROM
YOU.
#BEYOUNIQUE

July 7, 2014

The only person that is in your own way is you.

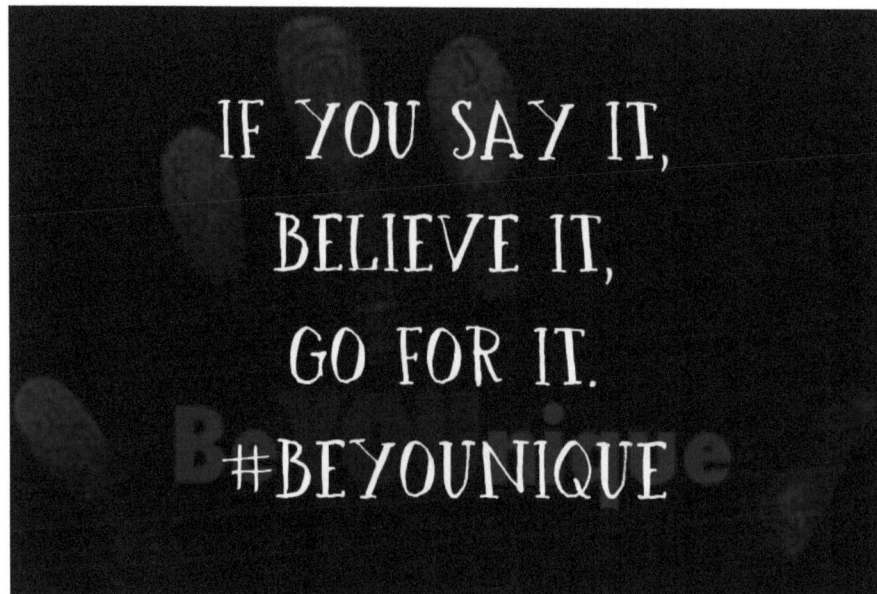

IF YOU SAY IT,
BELIEVE IT,
GO FOR IT.
#BEYOUNIQUE

July 8, 2014

The question is are you ready?

IF GOD CAN CREATE THE UNIVERSE IN
ONE TRILLIONTH OF A SECOND, THEN
HE CAN CHANGE YOUR LIFE AROUND
IN AN INSTANT.
#BEYOUNIQUE

July 10, 2014

I am beautiful.

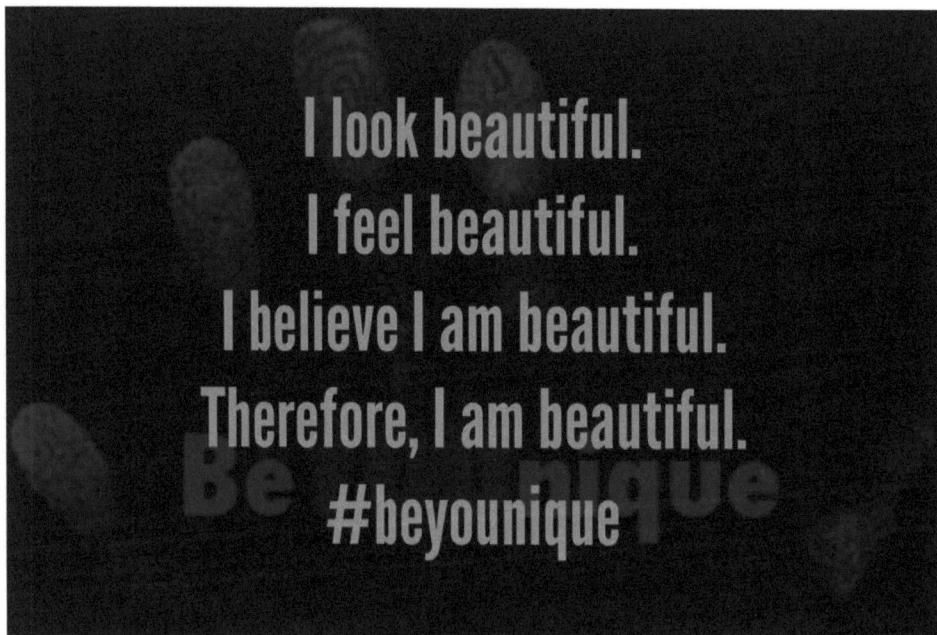

I look beautiful.
I feel beautiful.
I believe I am beautiful.
Therefore, I am beautiful.
#beyounique

July 11, 2014

#forgiveness #Godcanonlydothat #ohyeahedidthat #godslove #godisawesome #God
#mygodisable #missioncomplete #livinglife #lovingme #begreat #beautiful #beyounique

THE AWESOME TRUTH ABOUT GOD IS THAT HE HAS
ALREADY FORGIVEN ME FOR SINS I HAVEN'T EVEN
COMMITTED YET. HOW CAN THAT BE POSSIBLE?
ALL THINGS ARE POSSIBLE WITH GOD!
#BEYOUNIQUE

July 22, 2014

Today there are many things that boggled my mind when I woke up. But I chose to shift the atmosphere and meditate on Gods word and His promises.
Have a blessed day!

THERE WERE 130,745 PEOPLE WHO DIED TODAY AS OF 7:57PM. IF YOU'RE READING THIS TEXT ASK YOURSELF DID YOU ACCOMPLISH ONE OF YOUR GOALS TODAY? DID YOU DO ANYTHING TO GET YOU ONE STEP CLOSER TO YOUR GOAL? THERE WAS SOMEONE APART OF THAT 130,745 WHO DIDN'T GET A CHANCE TO.
WHAT ARE YOU WAITING FOR?
STOP PUTTING IT OFF AND GET STARTED NOW.
#BEYOUNIQUE

July 23, 2014

Right now the world is focused on social media and documenting their thoughts and life in its most precious form; from status updates to photos and now videos. Let me remind you that everything doesn't need to be documented. The things one sees on their timeline are just too much for the public. Keep something's to yourself. I don't want to know everything about you and I haven't seen you in ten years. Ladies leave something's to the imagination. I'm tired of seeing you bare it all... literally. Exude nothing but class at all times; especially when it comes to what you write. You're complaining about being single then you wonder why. Although you may not be speaking, you're posting and it should still exude life and not death. I'm not perfect but let's be cognizant of what we are putting out in the atmosphere. That goes for men too! Make it a great day!

Peace and blessings!

July 25, 2014

Just a thought.

We don't fall in love with flesh, we fall in love with the soul.
If God loves us supernaturally who says that we don't?
#beyounique

September 23, 2014

Just a small reminder: I am a flawed Queen waiting patiently for her King and I will adapt to any and every situation by the grace of God.

#letsnotgetittwisted #iwasalwaysroyalty #readyourbibleitsinthere #getrightorgetleft #ovo #queen #beyounique

September 28, 2014

I remember as a kid I was jealous of the kids who I thought were prettier than me. I was tall and skinny and felt out of place; never confident in who I was. It wasn't until I was in high school when I embraced who I was, curves and all. Although we have many things to be jealous of, we should know that the bible can help us. Be blessed.

September 29, 2014

At the end of the day God loves you more than anyone roaming His Earth. Never forget that. No man will ever love you more than you're Father in heaven.

There are too many women seeking love in all the wrong places, men too. I love love but I couldn't have gotten here without knowing who loves me first. When I think about it long enough I could cry. His love is like the waves of an ocean; never ending, constant, and consistent no matter what type of day it is. Whether you're going through a storm or experiencing a sunny day. His love remains the same. Embrace it.

#truth #lovingme #lovingmeuntilwe #marriagematerial #truthofthematteris #Godlovesmebest #iloveme #marriagegoals

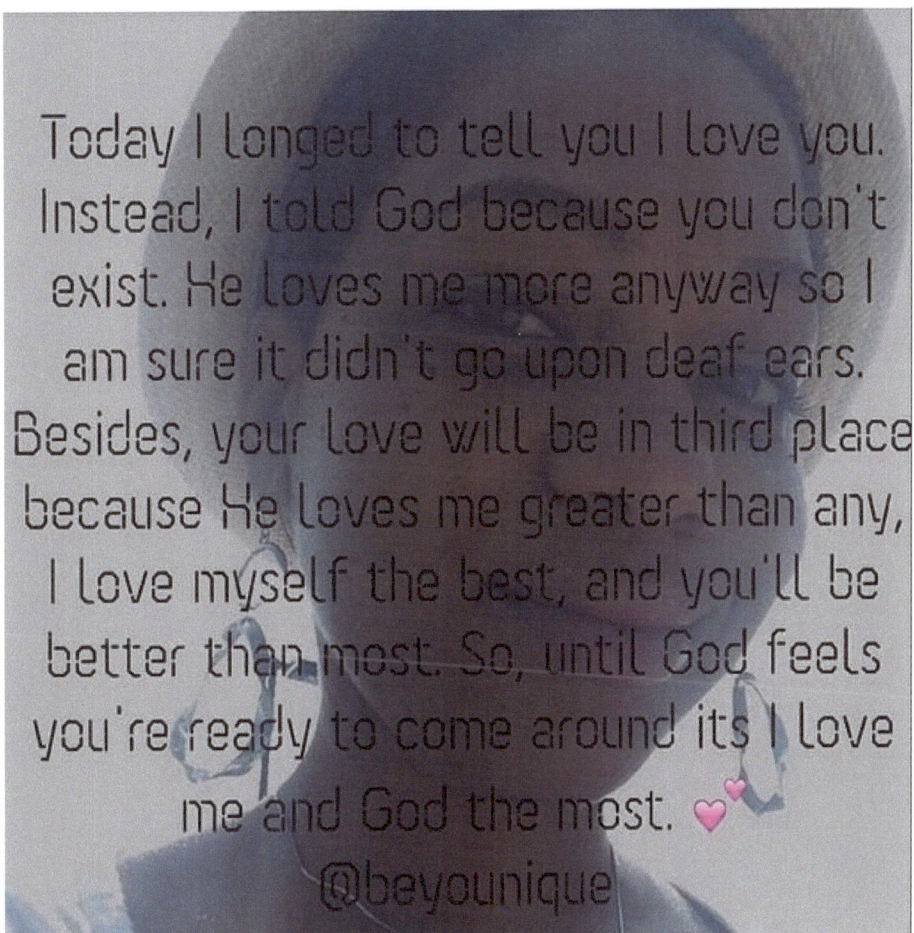

Today I longed to tell you I love you. Instead, I told God because you don't exist. He loves me more anyway so I am sure it didn't go upon deaf ears. Besides, your love will be in third place because He loves me greater than any, I love myself the best, and you'll be better than most. So, until God feels you're ready to come around its I love me and God the most. 💕
@beyounique

October 7, 2014

I hate that I have to even say this but whatev:

I'm so tired of hearing people say "don't stress yourself", "don't work too hard", "take it easy", "I don't know how you do it", "remember to take a break", "when do you sleep?" When you want something as bad as I do, then all of those things don't matter. I work hard and I play harder. Stop watching me and start making a difference. Don't worry about me, just watch. I no longer tell people what I'm doing, I just want you to see the result. So, keep your comments to yourself. You're not helping you're only trying to throw salt in the game.

#moveouttheway #justwatchandlearn #mycomebackisalwaysgreat #showingoutallmonth #ijs #destiny #blessed #ialreadywon #beyounique

October 20, 2014

Is my mic on? Growth has been the greatest asset I took out of the year 2013. When you know what you want you never settle for less. Stop emotionally tying yourself to people who you have no interest in. Be honest with yourself and others. It'll save you from awkward moments and conversations later. #honestyisthebestquality #godlysubmission #hisandhers #union #covenant #ido #growth #maturity #change #beyoutimes2

LOCKED
FROM THE MOMENT WE LOCKED EYES I KNEW MY FUTURE WOULD BE
NOTHING SHORT OF BLISS.
I SAW YOU, ME, THEN WE. MY FUTURE THAT ONCE CONSISTED OF
ONLY ME, NOW INCLUDED YOU AND A PARTY OF TWO.
IN A WORLD OF CHAOS YOU ARE THE EYE OF THE STORM AND ALL I
WANTED TO KNOW IS WHY IT TOOK YOU SO LONG...
#BEYOUNIQUE

October 28, 2014

Everyone is good at something. Don't let the next ten years pass you by and you wonder why some punk kid invented your invention and is now the next young millionaire. God trusted you with it first but you didn't want to listen. So I repeat, everyone is good at something. Don't let another day go by without you pursuing a dream God placed in YOUR heart!

#beyoutimes2

November 3, 2014

I kept seeing this post everywhere and just cracked up laughing because I could totally picture myself on the floor in tears thinking how great my God is. It amazes me when people say they don't even believe in a higher power. There are too many things that scientist cannot explain. I just love that the human body was created to do so many amazing things. For women alone to create life inside of her. Her entire body is physically changing so another human can develop - all because of God. My other favorite thing is why we have eyebrows; they look amazing when they are threaded or waxed but they are there to protect us from getting sweat in our eyes. Genius if you ask me. So, I can tell you what He has done for me in so many ways but He does so much daily it would be a disgrace if I didn't wake up and thank Him for his faithfulness. Thank you Lord for the little things and the greater things that I see as impossible but you see it as being possible with you. Xoxo. I love you forever!!!

#myGodisgreater #hallelujah #ilovemesomeGod #myLordreigns #shoutout #babyjesus #ybe #womeninbiz #entrepreneur #lovinglife #lovingme #love #beyoutimes2

November 3, 2014

The things I think about when I'm tired... Love and marriage.

#beyoutimes2

I thought about doing it a while ago but the time wasn't right. We've spent 13 hours, 2 minutes and 20 seconds together and then there it was... timing was right. I thought about a field of lilies, a warm sunny day in California, waves crashing on my feet and sand in between my toes, I thought about an extra hot caramel brûlée, and your hands playing in my hair; all the things that make me happy. Then you appeared. I said hello and you said hi back and all I wanted was a kiss and my heart back. 💕

November 5, 2014

Normal
nor·mal
ˈnôrməl/
adjective
1. conforming to a standard; usual, typical, or expected.

Don't be normal.

#beyoutimes2

IF YOU'RE CONSIDERED NORMAL YOU'RE NOT APPLYING YOURSELF TO YOUR FULLEST POTENTIAL.
#BEYOUTIME2

November 5, 2014

Sometimes love sneaks up on you. Other times you're forced down loves lane. If I had to choose again, I would choose honesty, not only is it the best quality but it's always done me the same. It's been without bounds or limits. It's never lied to me, cheated on me, or deceived me. It's always been real. I would always choose honesty... Question is could you say the same?
#beyounique

November 7, 2014

Think about it most people don't want to stay in a relationship because they do not like what the other person is dishing out. Yet, when the next person comes around they will deal with all of the bolog-na in the world because they hated "starting over" in the first place. Next thing you know it's three years later and they are married to this person. How? Why? Because they settled when they should've compromised with you. Compromise now because you probably have a pearl and you don't even know it. #relationships #lovelife #beyou #free #vulnerable #inlove #living #lovinglife #faith #be #befree #beinlove #compromise #neversettle #beyounique #beyoutimes2

COMPROMISE IS DIFFERENT FROM SETTLING.

November 9, 2014

Ladies, happiness doesn't have to include a man. You can make you happy. It all starts within.

#knowyourworth #iloveme #livelife #relationships #lovelife #beyou #befree #neversettle #faith #lovinglife #beyounique #beyoutimes2

The highest level of happiness can be experienced without having a man in your life.

November 9, 2014

I'll be honest. I don't like sharing. So when it's time you'll know because you don't have much of a choice to not give your all. You're either with it or you're not. It's all about honoring me when I'm with you and when I'm not and I will definitely do the same. Cheating is for boys and girls not men and women who are adults and ready to settle down. So, the question is: are you ready to honor me or do I need a list of cheat codes to figure out the game you're playing

#iwin #vulnerable #compromise #honorme #honor #love #faith #livelove #living #knowyourworth #iloveme #relationships #beyou #befree #neversettle #faith #lovinglife #beyounique #beyoutimes2

November 10, 2014

Giving is so much greater than receiving especially when giving to complete strangers. I remember watching Suzie Orman one day and she said when you donate clothing or anything give things that you want to keep the most. Anyone who knows me knows I love me some uggs and I don't care what you have to say about them they are warm, fuzzy, and cozy. I gave a slightly used pair to the homeless one year and said Id get a new pair and didn't. I missed them but I know someone appreciated them more. The following year I received a pair for Christmas and purchased a pair prior to Christmas. God will look out for you.

November 25, 2014

Period

You're never going to reach your greatest potential by never confronting your emotions.

Be YOU nique

1. AN IDEA OR VISION
2. DELIVERED BY GOD TO YOU
3. IT CAN BE SEEN, FELT, EVEN TASTED BUT,
4. IT WILL ONLY BECOME A REALITY ONCE YOU PUT IT INTO MOTION.
THIS IS THE DEFINITION OF A DREAM.
TAKE THE LAST STEP.
#BEYOUNIQUE

December 5, 2014

I've been so quiet about the next book. It's been such a challenge to put this one out. It's like a musician putting out a sophomore album. You try to duplicate the first time since it was so great but I have to take me out of it and continue to let God guide and control the process. I just wrote the books dedication and it made me weep a bit. It's so powerful what love can do. This book is about men but it'll be filled with much love.

God is love. There is nothing greater than love because it all begins and ends with love.

Right now love is this butter pecan gelato but when I wake up in five hours it'll be the gift of waking up if it is Gods will. Love is all around us. Take a minute to see it, admire it, adore it, take it all in. It's what God would want you to do. To see HIM in everything.

I grind so my children's children don't have to. Sacrificing sleep, a social life, and at times sanity is so worth it. I am not made to work for anyone but God. Sometimes submission is necessary because you will always need people to build and achieve your dream. My children however will have a ready made empire and guess what they too won't have to work for anyone because of the sacrifice that I have made. Mark my words...I am destined to make it further than I have ever imagined and so are you. It all starts with a dream and determination.

December 7, 2014

#rp but let me tell you, my grind is 7 days a week. Yes, I may be extremely behind on my favorite shows, yes, I may miss too many church services because I'm working but in 2015 it will all payoff. As my pastor says at the end of every service, your best has yet to come. My time is short here on this Earth so in the mean time I will do what I can to make a difference. Good morning!

#beyoutimes2

2013 WAS PRACTICE
2014 WAS THE WARM UP
2015 IS GAME TIME

December 16, 2014 at 9:57pm

I am not here to live a mediocre life. I want the best life God has for me.

- Nadia

www.ingramcontent.com/pod-product-compliance
Lightning Source LLC
Chambersburg PA
CBHW041053110426
42740CB00044B/47

* 9 7 8 0 6 9 2 4 5 2 7 7 6 *